Gluten Free

Slow Cooker Recipes

50 Delicious Crock Pot Recipes

for the Gluten Free Diet

By

Patrick Smith

ISBN-10: 1500369780
ISBN-13: 978-1500369781

Contents

A Word on the Recipes

Slow cooking is a way to make cooking easier and more convenient, because you need to do very little yourself. It is the slow cooker that does most of the work.

Many people think that a good slow cooker recipe consists mostly of a list of ingredients, a few simple preparation steps and the cooking time. However, be aware that many of the best slow cooker recipes require at least one more cooking step than just placing the ingredients in the cooker and letting it do its job.

Typically, this involves sautéing bacon, onions or other ingredients in a pan for a few minutes before adding them to the cooker. Please don't be surprised to find a few recipes that have such an additional step.

The purpose of this book is to give you good and interesting recipes, not just fast ones. As always when it comes to recipes, they are only a basis and can be altered. Feel free to cut out extra cooking steps if you wish or make changes according to your liking.

Four of the recipes in this book use gluten-free tortillas or tacos, and five recipes mention bread. For tortilla products, refer to the Mission® brand. All of their tortilla products are gluten-free. Also, there is a wide variety of gluten-free bread available, so you should not run into trouble finding any. Optionally, you can also make gluten-free bread yourself.

Many of the recipes include coconut products, such as coconut oil, coconut cream or coconut milk. In most cases, these are optional. If coconut products are new to you, then know they are some of the healthiest foods in the world and have countless benefits.

Now, let's get cooking!
Patrick Smith

Section 1: Breakfasts

1. Fruity Nut Breakfast

This steel cut oat breakfast contains fruits, nuts and coconut ingredients for rich flavor and many health benefits. It is very easy to prepare. If you are out of coconut products, which a healthy household should never be, you can also use regular butter and milk.

1 cup gluten-free **steel cut oats**
2 cups **milk** or **coconut milk**
1 tsp **butter** or **coconut butter**
2 cup **pear** (peeled, diced)
½ cup **walnuts** (diced)
½ cup **raisins** (diced)
¼ tsp. **salt**
½ tsp. **cinnamon**
1/4 cup **sugar** (optional)

Makes 8 servings
Calories: 118 per serving

Combine all of the ingredients in a slow cooker. Stir to combine.

Turn heat on low and cook for 6 hours. At this point, the oats should be tender. If not, let it cook for 1 more hour.

Stir before serving.

Enjoy!

2. Apple Cinnamon Dish

This breakfast is not only delicious, but also very easy to prepare and fills the house with a wonderful smell while it is cooking. It is best suited for a 5-quart (4.7 liter) or larger slow cooker, but you can easily scale it down.

2 **Granny Smith apples** (peeled, cored, diced)
22 oz. (625 ml) unsweetened **applesauce** or **apple juice**
1 ½ cups gluten-free **steel cut oats**
¼ cup **cinnamon** (ground)

Makes 10 servings
Calories: 137 per serving

Combine 8 cups water, the apple dices, either applesauce or apple juice, steel cut oats, and cinnamon in the slow cooker.

Set to low heat and cook for 5 hours and 45 minutes.

Enjoy!

3. Dutch Breakfast

I picked up this recipe when I lived in the Netherlands for a few years. It produces 12 servings, which is enough for the whole family and can easily be saved for the next day.

This recipe requires you to fry the result after the slow cooking. It is good if you are short on time, because you can slow cook the meal the day before, refrigerate it and simply fry it in the morning. This only takes a few minutes.

5 cups gluten-free **steel cut oats**
¼ cup **olive oil** or **coconut oil**
2 large **onions** (finely chopped)
2 lbs. (900 g) **beef** (ground)
2 lbs. (900 g) **pork sausage** (ground)
2 tsp salt and ground **black pepper**

Makes 12 servings
Calories: 125 per serving

Combine 12 cups of water, salt, pepper, onions, beef, pork, and steel cut oats in a slow cooker. Stir to combine. Cover, set heat to low and cook for 4 ½ hours.

Remove the mixture from the slow cooker and transfer to a baking pan. Allow to cool until partially solid, then refrigerate for 1 hour. At this point, the mixture should be solid.

Cut the solid mixture into slices. Heat the oil of your choice in a frying pan over medium heat and add the slices one at a time. Fry each slice until evenly browned.

Traditionally, this is served with fried eggs.

4. Dutch Slow Cooker Pancakes

I picked up this recipe when I lived in the Netherlands for a few years. These simple pancakes are a traditional breakfast in Germany and its neighbors.

It is originally made without coconut ingredients, but using them not only gives them extra taste, it also makes them healthier.

1 cup **arrowroot flour** or **coconut flour**
1 **cup milk** or **coconut milk**
6 **eggs**
1/2 tsp **salt**
4 tbs **butter** or **coconut butter**

Makes 6 servings
Calories: 87 per serving

Combine the flour of your choice, salt and eggs in a bowl. Stir to blend.

Melt the butter of your choice in a slow cooker on medium heat. Add the batter to the cooker, cover and set heat to high. Cook for 1 hour. At this point, the pancake should be puffed up.

You can serve this with syrup, honey, powdered sugar or coconut cream on top.

Enjoy!

5. Potato Bacon Breakfast

This potato recipe is not only great for breakfast, it goes well with almost anything and can be used as a side dish as well.

4 medium **potatoes** (cut)
5 **bacon** slices (cooked)
2 tbs **butter** or **coconut butter**
1 cup **Cheddar cheese** (shredded)
¼ cup **onion** (minced)
½ tsp **salt** and **pepper**

Makes 4 servings
Calories: 125 per serving

Cut the potatoes into bite sized pieces.

Make two layers of ingredients in a slow cooker. Cover the bottom with half of the potatoes, then top with half of the onion and the butter of your choice. Season with half of the salt and pepper, then top with half of the bacon and cheese. Make the second layer in the same way.

Set heat to low and cook for 9 hours, or 4 ½ hours on high heat.

Enjoy!

Section 2: Main Dishes

1. Tamari Pork

This is an Asian recipe that uses Tamari, a gluten-free Japanese soy sauce.

2.5 lbs. (1.1 kg) **pork**
½ tsp **Chinese Five Spice**
½ cup **rice wine vinegar**
4 cloves **garlic** (minced)
½ cup **chicken stock**
½ cup **Tamari**
1 **ginger** knob (grated)
1 tsp **red pepper flakes**
1 tsp **olive oil** or **coconut oil**
2 tbs **orange juice** (squeezed)
8 oz. (225 g) **mushrooms** (sliced)
1 lb. (450 g) **mustard greens**
Salt and **pepper**, to taste

Makes 8 servings
Calories: 230 per serving

Place the liquid ingredients, the red pepper flakes, garlic, mushrooms, spice and ginger in a slow cooker.

Season the pork with salt and pepper, then add it to the cooker.

Cover, set heat to low and cook for 7 hours. 15 minutes before the end of the cooking time, add the mustard greens to the cooker.

Remove the pork and shred it on a plate.

Add the greens to the pork mix and serve.

2. Chicken Cinnamon Tacos

This recipe shows that great taste, simplicity and health can go hand in hand. I recommend trying out coconut cream as a taco topping. It adds an exotic taste and has many health benefits.

Note: Mission® tortilla products are gluten-free.

2 lbs. (910 g) **chicken breast**
2 cloves **garlic**
2 **cinnamon sticks**
Coconut cream (optional)
1 **onion** (sliced)
15 oz. (425 g) **stewed tomatoes** (chopped)
3 **chipotle chili peppers**
6 Mission® gluten-free **Taco shells**
Salt to taste

Makes 6 servings
Calories: 220 per serving

Place the chicken breasts in a slow cooker. Add the tomatoes, chipotle chilies, garlic, onion and cinnamon sticks. Stir to coat.

Set to high heat and cook for 4 hours.

Remove the chicken, cinnamon and chipotle chilies. Use two forks to shred the chicken.

Return the shredded chicken meat to the slow cooker and stir.

Serve with gluten-free tacos. If you wish, add a taco topping of your choice. Personally, I like using coconut cream for this.

Enjoy!

3. Cranberry Beef

This roast is very easy to make. The cranberry sauce adds a gentle sweetness and produces and unforgettable taste overall.

4 lbs. (1.8 kg) **beef chuck roast**
30 oz. (850 g) **cranberry sauce**
3 cups **beef broth**
3 tbs **arrowroot flour** or **coconut flour**
2 tbs **olive oil** or **coconut oil**
2 **red onions** (chopped)
Salt and ground **black pepper**

Makes 10 servings
Calories: 365 per serving

For the sauce, pour 1 cup of water in a slow cooker over high heat. Add the beef broth and stir in the cranberry sauce until blended.

Evenly sprinkle the roast with the flour of your choice and season with salt and pepper. Add the roast and onion to the slow cooker.

Cover, set heat to low and cook for 8 hours until the roast is tender.

Serve with rice.

Enjoy!

4. Italian Tomato Meatballs

Most meatballs combine pork, beef and veal. This recipe uses a lighter sauce to intensify the flavor without adding much on calories and fat. As always, choose organic meat.

1 lb. (450 g) **lean beef** (ground)
2 lbs. (900 g) **chicken** or **turkey sausage** (ground)
1 **egg** and 1 **egg white**
1 tsp **salt**
1 **small onion** (minced)
6 **garlic cloves** (minced)
½ tbs **olive oil** or **coconut oil**
14 oz. (400 g) **dice tomatoes**
2 tsp **Italian seasoning**
1 **bay leaf**
¼ **parsley** (minced)
28 oz. (800g) **tomatoes** (crushed)
1 tsp **red pepper flakes**
1 cup **chicken broth**

Makes 8 servings
Calories: 210 per serving

Whisk the egg and egg white together in a bowl. Add the parsley, garlic cloves and ¼ of the onion.

Combine the beef and sausage and stir to mix. Roll the mixture into balls. It should be enough for 22-25 meatballs, depending on the size you make them. Place in a slow cooker.

Add the remaining ¾ of the onion, red pepper flakes, Italian seasoning, garlic, diced tomatoes, bay leaf, crushed tomatoes, and chicken broth to the slow cooker.

Pour the mixture in the bowl over the meatballs. Cover, set heat to low and cook for 6 hours.

5. Chicken and Cauliflower

This is a delicious Indian chicken dish with a lot of different flavors. Like many Indian recipes, it contains coconut ingredients.

1 lb. (450 g) **chicken breast** (cut into chunks)
1 lb. (450 g) **chicken thighs**
1 lb. (450 g) **cauliflower florets**
1 cup **coconut milk**
1 tbs **coriander**
1 tsp **salt**
2 whole **jalapeños**
1 **onion** (diced)
1 tbs **pepper**
3 inch (7.6 cm) **ginger** (grated)
1 tbs **arrowroot flour** or **coconut flour**
1 tbs **cumin**
2 tbs **coconut butter**
6 **garlic cloves** (minced)
3 tbs **garam masala**
4 cups **tomatoes** (crushed)

Makes 10 servings
Calories: 200 per serving

Season the chicken with the cumin, salt, and coriander. Place in a slow cooker.

Add the jalapeños, coconut butter, garlic, cauliflower, onion, tomatoes, garam masala, and ginger on top of the chicken.

Cover, set heat to low and cook for 6 hours until the chicken is tender.

10 minutes before the end of the cooking time, stir in the flour of your choice and coconut milk. Cover for 10 minutes until the sauce is thick.

6. Turkish Goulash

This is one of my favorite goulash recipes, given to me by my grandma when I first learned to cook. It can be served over rice or pasta of any kind.

2 lbs. (910 g) **beef chuck roast** (cubed)
¼ cup **arrowroot flour** or **coconut flour**
1 large **onion** (diced)
2 tbs **Worcestershire sauce**
2 tsp **sweet paprika**
½ tsp **dry mustard**
½ cup gluten-free **ketchup** (optionally self-made)
2 tsp salt

Makes 6 servings
Calories: 255 per serving

In a bowl, combine 1 cup water, ketchup, dry mustard, Worcestershire sauce, and paprika. Stir to blend.

Place the beef and onion in a slow cooker, then pour the sauce.

Cover, set heat to low and cook for 9 hours. At this point, the meat should be tender.

In a second bowl, combine the flour of your choice and ¼ cup of water. Pour into the slow cooker and stir. Continue cooking for 15 more minutes.

Serve over rice or pasta of any kind.

Enjoy!

7. Pork and Bean Casserole

In my experience, this sweet flavored dish tends to become an immediate favorite among those who try it, especially children.

30 oz. (850 g) canned **baked beans with pork**
1 ½ lbs. (680 g) **beef** (ground)
4 **bacon** slices
1 tbs **olive oil** or **coconut oil**
1 large **green bell pepper** (chopped)
½ cup gluten-free **ketchup** (optionally self-made)
¼ cup **molasses** or ½ cup **maple syrup**
1 tsp **dry mustard**
1 tsp **salt**
½ tsp **black pepper** (ground)

Makes 8 servings
Calories: 275 per serving

Optionally and for the best results, heat the oil of your choice in a frying pan over medium heat. Add the bacon slices and green bell pepper. Sauté for 6 minutes. Transfer to a slow cooker.

If you are short on time, you can also skip the step above and add the ingredients to the cooker directly.

Add the mustard, molasses or maple syrup, ketchup, pork and beans to the slow cooker. Season with salt and pepper. Stir to combine.

Cover, set heat to low and cook for 4 hours. Serve with gluten-free bread.

Enjoy!

8. Stuffed Cabbage

This recipe is for cabbage rolls stuffed with rice, onion, and ground beef. It is as much a treat as it is a meal. Because of this, it has additional steps other than slow cooking, so better make this on weekends when you have the extra time.

1 lb. (450 g) **beef** (ground)
1 cup **rice** (any, cooked)
8 oz. (225 g) **tomato sauce**
12 **cabbage** leaves (cooked)
1 **egg** (beaten)
¼ cup **milk** or **coconut milk**
¼ cup **onion** (minced)
1 tbs **lemon juice**
1 tbs **brown sugar** (optional)
1 tsp **Worcestershire sauce**
1 ¼ tsp **salt** and **black pepper** (ground)

Makes 6 servings
Calories: 230 per serving

Cook the rice according to package instructions.

Place cabbage leaves in a pot of boiling water. Cook for 3 minutes, then transfer to a plate.

In a bowl, combine the cooked rice with the beef, egg, milk of your choice, and onion. Season with salt and pepper.

Use ¼ cup of the meat mixture to roll into each cabbage leaf. Tuck in the sides of each leaf.

Place the leaf rolls in a slow cooker. In another bowl, combine the lemon juice, optional brown sugar, tomato sauce, and Worcestershire sauce. Pour into the slow cooker.

Cover, set heat to low and cook for 9 hours.

9. Sauerkraut and Sausage Party Dish

This is a simple recipe from Germany with few ingredients, but it is surprisingly good. I traditionally serve this on parties and New Year's Eve, where it is always a big hit and gone within an hour.

3 lbs. (1.36 kg) **beef smoked sausage** (ground or sliced)
2.5 lbs. (1.14 kg) **sauerkraut**
1/4 cup **brown sugar**
1 **onion** or **apple** (sliced)

Makes 10 servings
Calories: 335 per serving

Combine the sauerkraut and sugar in a slow cooker. Top with the onion and ground or sliced sausage.

Cover, set heat to high and cook for 2 hours. While cooking, add a bit of water if it gets too dry.

Reduce to low heat, then cook for 2 more hours.

Enjoy!

10. Pot Roast and Potatoes

This is a great base recipe and easy to modify. For example, you can use chuck top roast instead of the top sirloin roast, or you can add ¾ cup of red wine.

3 lbs. (1.36 kg) **top sirloin roast**
6 **potatoes** (quartered)
4 **carrots** (cut)
2 large **red** or **green bell peppers** (cut)
2 large **sweet onions** (chopped)
6 **garlic** cloves (slivered)
1 **bay leaf**
1 tsp **paprika**
½ cup **beef broth**
3 cubes **beef bouillon**
1 tsp **salt** and ground **black pepper**

Makes 8 servings
Calories: 320 per serving

Season the roast with paprika, salt and pepper. Cut slits into the roast and shove the garlic slivers into them.

Combine the potatoes, onions, and carrots in a slow cooker. Top with the roast. Add ½ cup water and beef broth, then add the bay leaf and bouillon cubes.

Cover, set heat to low and cook for 8 hours. Add the bell peppers 45 minutes before the end of the cooking time.

Enjoy!

11. Curry Lentil Meal

This fulfilling lentil meal is rich in ingredients and taste, yet it is cheap and easy to make.

4 cups **brown lentils**
4 cloves **garlic** (minced)
3 lbs. **tomatoes** (pureed)
4 ½ tbs **red curry paste**
2 **onions** (diced)
½ cup **milk** or **coconut milk**
1 tbs **ginger** (minced)
4 tbs **butter** or **coconut butter**
1 tbs **garam masala**
½ tsp **cayenne pepper**
1½ tsp **turmeric**
1 tsp **salt** and ground **black pepper**
Cilantro (for garnish)

Makes 12 servings
Calories: 265 per serving

Combine the lentils, onions, butter of your choice, curry, garlic, turmeric, cayenne, and ginger in a slow cooker. Stir to combine.

Add ½ of the tomato puree and 6 cups of water, or until ingredients are covered. Stir to combine.

Cover, set heat to low and cook for 8 hours, or 4 ½ on high heat. The lentils should be soft by the end.

While cooking, add more water if it gets too dry. Choose water amount depending on how soupy you want the meal to be.

Taste and season with salt and pepper as needed. Stir in the milk of your choice, then sprinkle with cilantro.

Serve with rice or gluten-free bread.

12. Apple Rosemary Pork

This is a very satisfying dish that combines the taste of apples and pork. It ranks among my personal favorite meals. Choose coconut oil over olive oil for the most health benefits.

3 lbs. (1.36 kg) **pork roast**
2 **apples** (peeled, cored, chopped)
1 tbs fresh **rosemary**
2 tbs **olive oil** or **coconut oil**
1 **onion** (chopped)
2 cloves **garlic** (crushed)
2 cups of **apple cider**
1 tsp fresh **thyme** (minced)
Salt and **pepper** (ground)

Makes 6 servings
Calories: 220 per serving

Heat the oil of your choice in a pan over medium heat. Add the pork and cook for 10 minutes until browned.

Transfer to a slow cooker, saving some of the oil. Place the onion in the pan, then cook for 5 minutes in the saved oil. Add the apples and garlic to the pan and cook for 5 more minutes. Transfer to the slow cooker.

Add the rest of the ingredients in the slow cooker. Cover, set heat to low and cook for 7 hours.

Taste and season with salt and pepper as needed.

Enjoy!

13. Quinoa Stuffed Peppers

Stuffed bell peppers are culinary Christmas presents. In my experience, this recipe is usually underestimated and comes as a surprise to most people.

4 **bell peppers** (any color)
½ cup **quinoa** (rinsed)
1 tsp **cumin**
2 cups **salsa**
1 tsp **garlic powder**
15 oz. (425 g) **black beans** (rinsed)
Cheddar cheese (grated, optional)
¾ tsp **salt**

Makes 4 servings
Calories: 165 per serving

Combine the salsa, quinoa, cumin, beans, optional Cheddar cheese, and garlic powder in a bowl, then season with salt. Stir to mix.

Cut the top off the bell peppers. Remove the seeds and membranes. Scoop the filling from the bowl into the peppers and replace the tops.

Place the peppers in a slow cooker. Cover, set heat to low and cook for 5 hours, or 3 hours on high heat.

Enjoy!

14. Slow Cooker Chili

No recipe repertoire would be complete without chili. After altering and testing many combinations, this turned out to be one of my favorite chili recipes.

3 lbs. (1.36 kg) **boneless pork shoulder** (cubed)
2 lbs. (910 g) **green salsa**
15 oz. (425 g) **black beans**
15 oz. (425 g) **tomatoes** (diced)
4 oz. (115 g) **jalapeños** (diced)
3 tbs **olive oil** or **coconut oil**
½ cup **onion** (chopped)
2 **garlic** cloves (minced)

Makes 8 servings
Calories: 245 per serving

Optionally and for the best results, heat the oil of your choice in a pan over medium heat. Add the garlic and onion, then cook for 5 minutes until the onion is translucent. Add the pork and cook on both sides until browned. Transfer to a slow cooker.

If you are short on time, you can also skip the steps above and place the ingredients in a slow cooker directly.

Add the tomatoes, black beans, green salsa, and jalapeños to the slow cooker.

Cover, set heat to low and cook for 6 hours, or 3 ½ hours on high heat.

Serve with rice.

Enjoy!

15. Floured Steak with Vegetables

This dish originated in Austria, where I learned it from a chef. It combines the juices of steak, tomatoes and carrots. If prepared in a slow cooker, it almost melts in your mouth.

2 lbs. (910 g) **round beef** (diced)
3 cups **tomatoes** (crushed)
4 **carrots** (cut)
4 **celery stalks** (cut)
¼ cup **arrowroot flour** or **coconut flour**
2 tbs **olive oil** or **coconut oil** (optional)
2 tsp **mustard powder**
1 medium **onion** (sliced)
3 **garlic cloves** (minced)
3 tbs **Worcestershire sauce**
1 tsp **sage**
1 tsp **thyme**
2 tsp **salt**
½ tsp **black pepper** (ground)

Makes 4 servings
Calories: 235 per serving

Combine the spices and the flour of your choice in a bowl. Season the beef with this spice mix.

Optionally and for the best results, heat the oil of your choice in a frying pan over medium heat. Add the beef to the pan and cook until browned. Transfer to a slow cooker.

If you are short on time, skip the step above and place the beef in the slow cooker directly.

Add the celery, onions, garlic, Worcestershire sauce tomatoes, and carrots to the slow cooker.

Cover, turn heat to low and cook for 8 hours.

16. Satsuma Turkey

The oranges and marmalade in this recipe provide a sweet and tangy flavor, while the pepper adds a spicy kick. Since turkey is always a bit more involved, there are some extra cooking steps in this recipe. It is not a dish for busy days.

3 cups **red onions** (thinly sliced)
2/3 cup fresh **orange juice**
2 tsp **tamarind paste**
60 oz. (1.7 kg) bone-in **turkey thighs** (skinned)
2 cups fresh **mandarin orange** (sectioned)
1/3 cup **orange marmalade**
½ tsp **red pepper** (crushed)
2 tsp **five spice powder**
1 tbs **olive oil** or **coconut oil**
1 ½ tbs **arrowroot flour** or **coconut flour**
1 tsp **salt**

Makes 8 servings
Calories: 280 per serving

Combine the red onions, orange juice, marmalade, tamarind paste and red pepper in a slow cooker.

Rinse the turkey thighs and dry. Season with spices. Heat the oil of your choice in a pan over medium heat. Add the turkey thighs to the pan and cook for 3 minutes on each side until browned.

Place the turkey thighs in a single layer over the onion mixture. Add the orange sections and cover. Cook for 4 hours on low heat.

Remove the turkey thighs from the slow cooker, then remove the bones and discard. Transfer to a plate.

To make a sauce, pour ¾ of the cooking liquid and orange sections into a pan.

Combine the flour of your choice and the remaining ¼ of the cooking liquid in a bowl. Whisk until smooth. Add flour mixture to the pan.

Bring the sauce to a boil and cook for 1 minute, stirring continuously until it thickens.

Pour sauce over turkey and serve.

Enjoy!

17. Venison Apple Roast

This recipe combines the juiciness and flavor or venison with apples, creating an irresistible meal. You can also use this recipe for other meat, if you don't want to use game.

3 lbs. (1.36 kg) boneless **venison roast**
1 large **apple** (cored, quartered)
1 tbs **olive oil** or **coconut oil**
2 small **onions** (sliced)
1 cube **beef bouillon**
4 **garlic** cloves (crushed)
Salt and ground **pepper**

Makes 8 servings
Calories: 195 per serving

Heat the oil of your choice in a slow cooker over medium heat. Add the venison, then cover with garlic, onions, and the apple.

Cover, set heat to low and cook for 7 hours. At this point, the venison should be tender. Remove and place on a platter.

For a sauce, add 1 cup water and the bouillon cube in the slow cooker. Bring to a boil while stirring. Fill into a gravy boat.

Enjoy!

18. Indian Curry Chicken

Coconuts are still a new ingredient in the western kitchen. In India, however, it has been used for a very long time. Indian cuisine is fabulous, not only for its use of curry, but since coconut products are a normal ingredient in it.

4 skinless, boneless **chicken thighs** (bite-sized cuts)
1 ½ oz. (45g) **butter** or **coconut butter**
2 tbs **olive oil** or **coconut oil**
14 oz. (400 ml) **coconut milk**
5 oz. (140 g) **tomato paste**
1 **onion** (diced)
3 **garlic** cloves (minced)
1 tsp **garam masala**
1 tbs **Indian curry paste**
2 tsp **tandoori masala**
2 tsp **curry powder**
14 **green cardamom pods**
1 cup **plain yoghurt**
Salt to taste

Makes 6 servings
Calories: 225 per serving

Place the tomato paste, onion, garlic, chicken, curry paste, curry powder, garam masala, tandoori masala, and garam masala in a slow cooker. Stir in the coconut milk, cardamom pods, and yoghurt, then season with salt.

Cover, set heat to low and cook for 7 hours, or 5 hours on high heat. At this point, the chicken should be tender.

Remove from the cooker and discard the cardamom pods.

Enjoy!

19. Sloppy Joe

Sloppy Joes are sandwiches that make delicious and quick meals. This dish is not only good for sandwiches, it also goes well with pasta, rice, potatoes and brown rolls. Don't forget to use gluten-free sandwich bread!

2 lbs. (910 g) **lean beef** (ground)
1 **onion** (chopped)
1 tbs **olive oil** or **coconut oil**
1 **green bell pepper** (chopped)
1 cup **tomato sauce**
2 tsp **chili powder**
1 tbs **steak seasoning**
3 **garlic cloves**
1 tbs **Worcestershire sauce**
1 cup **ketchup**
2 tbs **tomato paste**
1 tsp **mustard**
Salt to taste

Makes 8 servings
Calories: 230 per serving

Optionally and for the very best result, heat the oil of your choice in a pan over medium heat. Add the ground beef and cook until browned. Transfer to a slow cooker.

If you are short on time, add the beef to the cooker directly.

In a large bowl, combine the rest of the ingredients to make sauce. Pour over the beef and stir to combine.

Cover, set heat to low and cook for 8 hours, then set aside for 5 minutes before serving.

Enjoy!

20. Mexican Black Beans and Coconut

Black beans are one of the most popular Mexican ingredients. This dish can be served after cooking for 10 hours. I usually combine it with the exotic taste and health benefits of coconuts by topping the dish with coconut cream.

16 oz. (450 g) **black beans** (dried)
2 cups **onion** (chopped)
1 tbs **lime juice**
½ cup fresh **cilantro** (chopped)
3 cups (700 ml) **chicken broth**
1 tbs **chipotle chili** (chopped)
4 **garlic cloves** (minced)
4 oz. (110 g) **coconut cream** (optional)
½ cup **pumpkin seeds** (not salted)
1 tsp **salt**

Makes 14 servings
Calories: 160 per serving

Wash and drain the beans. Place in a slow cooker and pour water until it covers the beans completely. Add the broth, chopped onion, chipotle, salt, and garlic cloves. Stir to mix.

Cover, set heat to low and cook for 10 hours.

Add the lime juice. Mash the bean mixture until soft and thick. Top with the pumpkin seeds, cilantro and optional coconut cream.

Enjoy!

Section 3: Soups

Soups are a lot more involved than meals, usually requiring additional steps or being done in less than an hour. Slow cooker enthusiasts like me, however, still use their favorite slow cooker for these recipes.

1. Hot Pumpkin Soup

This recipe shows that great taste, simplicity and health can go hand in hand. It adds an exotic taste and has many health benefits.

1 tbs **olive oil** or **coconut oil**
½ tsp **cumin** (ground)
1 tbs fresh **cilantro** (chopped)
5 medium **red potatoes** (peeled, diced)
4 **garlic cloves** (minced)
1 **jalapeño** (diced, cored, seeded)
1 **Cubanelle** or **roasted green chili** (diced, cored, seeded)
4 cups **vegetable broth**
15 oz. (425 g) can **pumpkin** or **squash**
15 oz. (425 g) can **black beans** (rinsed, drained)
Salt and **fresh ground pepper**
Coconut milk to taste (optional)

Makes 4 servings
Calories: 235 per serving

Place the oil of your choice in a slow cooker, then add the pepper and spices. Stir to coat and cook for 5 minutes.

Add the garlic and stir again, then add the rest of the ingredients.

Lower the heat, cover and cook for 30 minutes until the potatoes are tender.

Test the taste and add seasoning as needed. Optionally, add a dash of coconut milk to taste.

Sprinkle with cilantro and serve. You can also serve this with Mission® gluten-free tortillas to dip.

Enjoy!

2. Spicy Coconut Pea Soup

This is a very healthy vegan-friendly recipe with great taste and extra spice due to the use of jalapeños.

3 **garlic cloves** (chopped)
1/3 cup **pickled jalapeños** (drained, chopped)
½ tsp **Old Bay Seasoning**
2 cups **split peas** (rinsed)
1 14-oz. (400 ml) can **coconut milk**
5 cups **vegetable broth**
1 tsp mild or hot **curry paste** to taste
½ tsp **red pepper chili flakes** to taste
Salt and ground **pepper** to taste

Makes 4 servings
Calories: 180 per serving

Bring water to a boil in your slow cooker. Add the peas to the cooker, cover and turn on low heat. Cook for 1 hour, then drain.

Return the peas into the slow cooker and add garlic, curry, seasoning, vegetable broth and pepper flakes.

Stir and bring the mixture to a simmer, then cook for about 1 hour. The peas should be tender and break apart easily at this point.

Add the coconut milk and stir. Simmer to reduce the amount of liquid. Keep doing so until the soup is as thick as you want it to be. If more liquid is needed, add some water.

Serve with jalapeños in the middle of the soup.

3. Potato Chicken Soup

This is a spicy soup with a lot of good ingredients that make it tasty and colorful to look at. I prefer the coconut oil over olive oil because of its natural taste and health benefits.

2 tbs **olive oil** or **coconut oil**
4 **split chicken breasts** (rinsed)
8 **garlic cloves** (chopped)
2 cups **cabbage** (shredded)
1 tsp **rubbed sage**
1 tsp of **oregano, dried basil** and **parsley**
1 **green bell pepper** (cored, seeded)
1 **yellow summer squash** (cut)
2 **zucchini squash** (cut)
7 **sweet potatoes**
4 oz. (115 g) **green chilies** to taste (chopped)
14 oz. (400 g) **Muir Glen organic tomatoes**
2 cups **organic chicken broth**
Salt and ground **pepper** to taste

Makes 4 servings
Calories: 250 per serving

Coat a slow cooker with the oil of your choice. Place the chicken breasts in it and top with garlic. Season with salt and pepper.

Combine the cabbage, summer squash, zucchini, bell pepper, sweet potatoes and green chilies in a bowl. Season with salt, pepper and herbs, then toss to coat.

Add the seasoned vegetable mix to the slow cooker and pour the chicken broth. The liquid in the cooker should cover everything. If it doesn't, you can add some more broth.

Cover and cook on high heat for 6 hours. At this point, the chicken should be tender and break apart. Adjust seasoning as needed.

4. Vegetable Lime Soup

This soup is light, lean and full of vegetables. As usual, I prefer the coconut oil over olive oil because of its natural taste and health benefits.

2 tbs **olive oil** or **coconut oil**
1 medium **red onion** (diced)
4 **garlic** cloves (chopped)
2 medium **zucchini squash** (trimmed, sliced, quartered)
2 medium **carrots** (chopped)
1 cup **cabbage** (shredded)
28 oz. (800 g) **organic tomatoes**
3 cups **vegetable broth**
1 tbs **parsley** and **basil** (both chopped)
Salt and fresh ground **pepper** to taste
1 **lime** (juice)

Makes 4 servings
Calories: 220 per serving

Coat the bottom of a slow cooker with the oil of your choice. Add the vegetables, then stir to mix.

Add the broth and make sure it covers all of the vegetables. Season with salt, pepper and herbs. You can also add some red pepper flakes, if you want the result to be hot.

Cover and cook for 6 hours on low heat.

Add the fresh lime juice, stir for 10 minutes and serve.

Enjoy!

5. Turkey Soup

Turkey soup is a special treat and always a delight. This dish proves again that healthy food and good taste can go hand in hand.

1 ½ lb. (680 g) **turkey breast** (skin on)
½ medium **winter squash** (peeled, cubed)
4 large **carrots** (sliced)
2 **celery ribs** (trimmed, chopped)
Salt and ground **pepper** to taste
3 **garlic cloves** (chopped)
Basil, **rosemary**, **thyme** or **marjoram** to taste
1 tbs **balsamic vinegar**
½ **red onion** (finely divided)
Parsley (chopped)

Makes 4 servings
Calories: 250 per serving

Place the turkey breast in a slow cooker. Top with onion, celery, squash, garlic and carrots. Season with salt, pepper and the herbs of your choice, then add the vinegar.

Pour water over the mix until all ingredients are submerged. Cover, set to high heat and cook for 5 hours. At this point, the turkey should be tender and easily break apart.

Remove the skin from the turkey and discard. Shred the turkey with forks.

Sprinkle with parsley and serve.

Enjoy!

6. African Bean and Potato Soup

This soup is rich in legumes and has a satisfying taste, especially if you choose to add peanut butter. I prefer the coconut oil over olive oil because of its natural taste and health benefits.

1 tbs **olive oil** or **coconut oil**
1 quart (1 liter) **vegetable broth**
2 tbs fresh **cilantro** (chopped)
1/2 tsp **cinnamon**
1 medium **red onion** (peeled, diced)
4 **garlic cloves** (minced)
1 medium **sweet potato** (peeled, diced)
1 large **yellow bell pepper** (cored, seeded, diced)
1 **jalapeño** (seeded, diced)
1 **lime** (juice)
1 tbs **red** or **green Thai Kitchen curry paste**
14 oz. (400 g) **white beans** (rinsed)
14 oz. (400 g) **black-eyed peas** (rinsed)
14 oz. (400 g) **black beans** (rinsed)
½ cup **peanut butter** (optional)
Salt and **black pepper** to taste

Makes 4 servings
Calories: 260 per serving

Pour the oil of your choice in a slow cooker and heat it over medium heat. Add the cinnamon and curry, then stir to mix.

Add the garlic, potato, onion, jalapeño and yellow pepper. Stir and cook for 6 minutes.

Add the beans and black-eyed peas, optional peanut butter and cilantro.

Cover and simmer for 30 minutes, until the vegetables are all tender. Stir in the fresh lime juice, then season with salt and pepper.

Let it simmer for 2 minutes and taste if the seasoning suits you. Adjust seasoning as needed.

Enjoy!

7. Tomato Soup

This is my standard recipe for tomato soup. It is perfect for lunch or as entry for dinner and has a great taste whether it is served hot or cold.

28 oz. (800 g) **tomatoes** (cored)
½ **onion**, (chopped)
2 cups **vegetable broth**
1/2 cup **white wine**
2 tbs **tomato paste**
2 tsp **dried basil**
½ tsp **cumin** (ground)
2/3 cup **almond milk** or **coconut milk**
1 tsp **salt**
¼ tsp **black pepper** (ground)

Makes 5 servings
Calories: 150 per serving

Place all ingredients except the milk of your choice in a slow cooker. Cover, set to low heat and cook for 4 hours.

Remove and add to a blender. Let it cool for 30 minutes. When cooled, blend completely.

Pour into a saucepan and add the milk of your choice. Heat but don't boil.

Serve with crackers or croutons.

Enjoy!

8. Quinoa Chicken Soup

This hearty soup is easy to make and perfect on cold days. It uses Quinoa, which has a lot of protein and quickly fills you up. Personally, I choose the poblano peppers over the bell peppers.

This recipe freezes very well. I like making large batches and keep them frozen for quick meals in the future.

2 lb. (900 g) **chicken thighs** (boneless, skinless)
2 **poblano peppers** or 1 **bell pepper** (chopped)
1 cup **quinoa** (any kind)
½ tsp **thyme** (dried)
3 **carrots** (chopped)
1 **onion** (chopped)
3 cups **kale** (chopped)
3 ribs **celery** (chopped)
8 cups **chicken broth**
6 **garlic cloves** (minced)
½ tsp **cumin**
Salt and **cayenne pepper** to taste

Makes 8 servings
Calories: 250 per serving

Place the chicken thighs in a slow cooker. Add the other ingredients on top. Make sure everything is covered by the chicken broth.

Cover, set heat to low and cook for 8 hours. At this point, the chicken should be so tender that it almost melts in your mouth.

Taste test and season with salt and pepper.

Enjoy!

9. Red Bean Rice Soup

Rice is an ingredient that can be eaten with almost anything. Since there are many types of rice, there is so much variety that it never gets boring. Mixing soups and rice always works.

30 oz. (850 g) **red beans** (rinsed)
20 oz. (570 g) any **sausage** (cut)
3 **bay leaves**
1 large **onion** (chopped)
2 tsp **olive oil** or **coconut oil**
1 tsp **oregano** (dried)
1 tbs **garlic** (finely minced)
2 tsp **thyme** (dried)
1 tbs **creole seasoning**
8 cups **chicken broth**
2 tbs **Worcestershire sauce**
2 tsp **green tabasco sauce**
2 cups any **rice** (cooked)

Makes 8 servings
Calories: 230 per serving

Heat the oil of your choice a slow cooker. Add the onion and sauté for 5 minutes, until it starts browning. Add the garlic, oregano, thyme, creole seasoning and sauté for 3 more minutes.

Rinse and drain canned beans and add to the slow cooker, then add the sausage cuts as well. Add the chicken broth, green Tabaco, Worcestershire sauce, and bay leaves. Set to low heat and cook for 8 hours, or 4 hours on high heat.

Before the soup is done, cook the rice of your choice according to package directions or using a rice cooker. If the soup is too thick, add more chicken broth and cook on high for 20 more minutes.

Serve with rice.

10. Red Lentil Spinach Coco Soup

This is one of my coconut recipes, using coconut oil and coconut milk. Both have a very good taste and a lot of health benefits. The red lentils, spinach and other ingredients make for an excellent soup after a long day or workout.

1 ½ cup **red lentils** (rinsed)
4 cups fresh **spinach** (chopped)
1 tbs **coconut oil**
2 cups **coconut milk**
1 large **onion** (chopped)
1 tsp **turmeric** (ground)
2 tsp **garlic** (minced)
1 tsp **coriander seed** (ground)
1 tsp **cumin** (ground)
½ tsp **Garam Masala**
1 tsp **cinnamon** (ground)
4 cups **vegetable broth**
Salt and ground **black pepper** to taste

Makes 5 servings
Calories: 240 per serving

Heat the coconut oil in a slow cooker over medium heat. Add the chopped onion and cook for 5 minutes, until it starts browning. Add the garlic, coriander, turmeric, cumin, cinnamon, and Garam Masala and cook for 3 more minutes.

Check the red lentils and remove any with discolorations. Rinse the lentils, then add them and the vegetable broth to the cooker. Set to low heat and cook for 4 hours, or 2 hours on high heat.

Set the heat to low, then add the spinach and coconut milk. Cook for 30 more minutes. Season with salt and pepper to your liking.

Optionally, serve with Greek yoghurt.

11. Cabbage Soup

Cabbage soup is a classic meal on days you are not feeling well. It is a healthy pick-me-up, easy to make, and is enough for several meals.

1 ½ lb. (690 g) **green cabbage** (cored, thinly sliced)
1 tbs **olive oil** or **coconut oil**
2 medium **carrots** (diced)
1 medium **red potato** (diced)
2 tsp **apple cider vinegar**
2 **yellow onions** (diced)
2 **garlic cloves** (minced)
3 **celery stalks** (sliced)
1 tbs **thyme leaves** (chopped)
6 cups **chicken broth**
2 **bay leaves**
Salt and ground **black pepper** to taste

Makes 6 servings
Calories: 210 per serving

Heat the oil of your choice in a slow cooker over medium heat. Add the onion and garlic and cook for 5 minutes.

Add the carrots, potato and celery, and cook for another 5 minutes. Stir in the thyme, then season with salt and pepper.

Add the chicken broth, vinegar, and bay leaves. Set to low heat and cook for 8 hours, or 5 hours on high heat.

Discard the bay leaves before serving.

Enjoy!

12. Mushroom Potato Soup

Mushrooms are among the healthiest foods in the world. They are medicinal foods and can do truly amazing things for your immune system. Because of this, I eat mushrooms regularly. Different mushrooms have vastly different benefits, so it is a good idea to mix it up. This adds variety as well.

1 lb. (450 g) **red potatoes** (cubed)
8 oz. (225 g) any edible **mushrooms** (sliced)
2 tbs **olive oil** or **coconut oil**
1 cup **coconut milk**
1 **tomato** (pureed)
5 **garlic cloves** (minced)
½ **red onion** (chopped)
¼ cup **curry powder**
1 tsp **coriander**
1 tsp **cumin**
1 tsp **sweet paprika**
½ **red bell pepper** (chopped)
½ tsp **chili powder**
¼ cup **green onions** (diced)

Makes 4 servings
Calories: 195 per serving

Heat the oil of your choice in a slow cooker over medium heat. Add the onion and red bell pepper, then cook for 5 minutes.

Add the garlic and cook for another 2 minutes. Add the mushrooms of your choice.

In a blender, spice grinder or food processor, blend the coriander, paprika, chili powder, cumin, and curry powder. Add this mix to the slow cooker.

Add the coconut milk and tomato puree to the slow cooker, then cover and cook for 50 minutes. At this point, the potatoes should be tender.

Optionally, use an immersion blender to puree the soup.

Garnish with the green onions and use gluten-free bread for dipping.

Enjoy!

13. Mexican Chicken Soup

This one of my favorite Mexican soups. It has many ingredients that perfectly join together.

3 cups **chicken** (shredded)
2 **tomatillos** (husked)
3 **garlic cloves** (minced)
1 tbs **olive oil** or **coconut oil**
1 cup **milk** (soy, regular or coconut)
2 **serrano chilies** (sliced)
2 **jalapeños** (sliced)
1 **red onion** (diced)
¼ cup fresh **cilantro**
4 oz. canned **green chilies** (diced)
2 cups **chicken broth**
1 **lime** (juiced)
1 tsp **chili powder**
1 tsp **cumin**
½ tsp **salt** and **black pepper**

Makes 4 servings
Calories: 254 per serving

Optional step for the best results: Place the jalapeños, serrano chilies and tomatillos on a baking sheet and into the oven below the broiler. Set high heat a bake for 5 minutes, until the jalapeños and chilies start to blacken. Remove from oven and allow to cool.

If you are short on time, skip the step above.

Put your chosen oil in a slow cooker and heat it over medium heat. Add the garlic and onions, then cook for 6 minutes. Add the onions and garlic.

Peel the jalapeños and tomatillos, chop them and add them to the slow cooker.

Add the chicken broth, milk of your choice, green chilies, lime juice, cumin, and chili powder. Season with salt, pepper and cilantro.

Cook for 5 minutes, then add the chicken. Stir to mix, cover and simmer on low for 20 minutes.

Optionally, top with Mission® gluten-free tortillas or cilantro before serving.

Enjoy!

14a. Taco Seasoning

This taco seasoning can be used for any taco related meal, specifically in recipe 14b.

1 tsp **kosher salt**
1 tsp **cayenne pepper**
1 tbs **onion powder**
1 tbs **garlic powder**
1 tbs **coconut oil** (melted)
1 tbs **chili powder**
1 tbs **cumin** (ground)
1 tbs **onion powder**
1 tbs **garlic powder**
1 tbs **paprika**
1 tbs **oregano**

Makes 7 servings
Calories: 30 per serving

Melt the coconut oil in a frying pan on low heat, or use a warmed cup. Coconut oil melts in your hand almost instantly, so very little heat is required.

Combine these ingredients in a bowl and use it to season your gluten-free tacos.

Enjoy!

14b. Beef and Bean Tacos

This recipe combines Beef, legumes and the homemade taco seasoning from recipe 14a. It can be used as a filling for tacos or as soup.

Note: Mission® tortilla products are gluten-free.

2 lbs. (910 g) **beef** (ground)
30 oz. (850 g) **pinto beans**
15 oz. (425 g) **kidney beans**
30 oz. (850 g) **diced tomatoes**
4 oz. (115 g) **green chilies**
15 oz. (425 g) **corn**
1 **red onion** (diced)
3 tbs **taco seasoning** from recipe 14a

Makes 7 servings
Calories: 255 per serving

Place the corn, chilies and tomatoes in a slow cooker. Prepare the seasoning from recipe 14a.

Add the beef and onion to the slow cooker, then add the seasoning. Stir to mix.

Set to low heat and cook for 9 hours, or 4 ½ hours on high heat.

Serve as soup or with Mission® gluten-free tacos.

Enjoy!

15. Beefy Pasta Soup

Beans, pasta, beef and tomatoes are already a great mix. Together with the other ingredients, this dish is amazing and always a hit. It doesn't sound like soup, but it has a lot of liquid and is eaten with a spoon.

2 lbs. (900 g) **beef** (ground)
8 oz. (225 g) **corn penne pasta**
2 lbs. (900 g) **tomato sauce**
30 oz. (850 g) **tomatoes** (diced)
15 oz. (425 g) **northern beans**
15 oz. (425 g) red **kidney beans**
1 **onion** (chopped)
1 cup **carrots** (chopped)
1 cup **celery** (chopped)
1 tsp **oregano**
1 tsp **basil**
1 tsp **rosemary**
2 cups **beef broth**
1 tbs **white vinegar**
1 ½ tsp **salt**
½ tsp **black pepper**

Makes 8 servings
Calories: 275 per serving

Place the carrots, celery, and onion in a slow cooker over medium heat. Cook for 5 minutes, then add the beef, basil, and rosemary. Season with salt and pepper.

Once the beef is browned, add the beans, tomato sauce and tomatoes. Stir to mix, then add the white vinegar and beef broth. Stir to mix.

Bring to a simmer, cover and cook on low heat for 8 hours, or 4 hours on high heat.

20-25 minutes before the cooker is done, prepare the penne pasta according to package directions.

Enjoy!

Section 4: Side Dishes

1. Potato Side Dish

There are a million ways to prepare potatoes. After testing many different ingredient combinations, I ended up with this recipe and have been using it for years.

2 ½ lbs. (1.15 kg) **Russet potatoes**
½ cup **butter** or **coconut butter** (melted)
1 tbs **lemon juice**
1 tbs **parsley** (dried)
2 **green onions** (sliced)
3 tsp **dill** (dried)
¼ tsp **salt** and **black pepper**

Makes 9 servings
Calories: 140 per serving

Cut the potatoes into wedges, then place in a slow cooker. Add ½ cup water.

Cover, set heat to low and cook for 6 hours until the potatoes are tender. Drain all liquid and return the potatoes to the cooker.

Add the butter of your choice, green onions, lemon juice, and seasoning. Toss to coat.

Serve the potatoes out of the cooker so they remain hot.

Enjoy!

2. Apple Cranberry Squash

This dish is almost like a dessert and great for all occasions, such as Christmas or Thanksgiving.

3 lbs. (1.36 kg) **butternut squash** (peeled, seeded, cubed)
5 **apples** (peeled, cored, chopped)
¾ cup **cranberries** (dried)
½ **white onion**, (diced, optional)
1 tbs **cinnamon** (ground)
1 ½ tbs **nutmeg** (ground)

Makes 10 servings
Calories: 135 per serving

Combine the apples, cranberries, squash, optional onion, nutmeg and cinnamon in a slow cooker.

Cover and set heat to low. Cook for 7 hours, or 4 hours on high heat. At this point, the squash should be tender.

Enjoy!

3. White Beans and Beef

This dish is nutritious and rich in flavor. I learned it from a Turkish friend, who told me it is a typical meal in Turkish households.

1 ½ cups **white kidney beans**
2 tbs **olive oil** or **coconut oil**
3 medium **onions** (chopped)
1 tbs **pimento sauce**
3 **garlic** cloves (chopped)
15 oz. (425 ml) **beef broth**
1 tbs **lemon juice**
3 tbs **tomato paste**
1 tsp **cumin** (ground)
Salt and **pepper** to taste

Makes 6 servings
Calories: 210 per serving

Heat the oil of your choice in a slow cooker over medium heat. Add all of the ingredients and season with salt and pepper. Stir to coat.

Cover, set heat to low and cook for 9 hours, or 6 hours on high heat. At this point, the mixture should be thick and the white beans tender.

Enjoy!

4. Turkey Stuffing

This recipe can be used as a side dish or as stuffing for Thanksgiving. It is surprisingly easy to make and yet one of the best stuffings I have ever tasted.

11 oz. (310 g) **mushrooms** (sliced)
12 cups gluten-free **bread cubes**
1 cup **butter** or **coconut butter**
2 cups **onion** (chopped)
2 cups **celery** (chopped)
2 **eggs** (beaten)
2 ½ cups **chicken broth**
¼ cup **fresh parsley** (chopped)
1 ½ tsp **sage** (dried)
1 tsp **thyme** (dried)
1 tsp **poultry seasoning**
1 ½ tsp **salt**
½ tsp **pepper** (ground)

Makes 15 servings
Calories: 218 per serving

Heat the butter of your choice in a frying pan over medium heat. Add the celery, onion, parsley, and mushrooms. Cook for 10 minutes and stir frequently.

Remove and combine with the gluten-free bread cubes in a large bowl. Add the poultry seasoning, thyme, sage, salt and pepper to the bowl, then add the chicken broth.

Note: If you are using hard packaged bread cubes from the store, add ½ extra cup of broth to make sure it is well moistened.

Transfer to a slow cooker, cover and cook on low heat for 4 hours.

Enjoy!

5. Spicy Black-Eyed Peas

This spicy dish is perfect for barbecues and Mexican dishes. It has a rich flavor and very little cholesterol. To spice it up more, you can safely add a whole jalapeño and double the cayenne pepper.

1 lb. (450 g) **black-eyed peas** (rinsed)
2 **garlic cloves** (diced)
8 oz. (225 g) **ham** (diced)
1 **red bell pepper** (stemmed, seeded, diced)
1 cube **chicken bouillon**
1 **onion** (diced)
½ **jalapeño** (seeded, minced)
4 **bacon slices** (chopped)
¼ tsp **cayenne pepper**
1 ½ tsp **cumin**
Salt and ground **black pepper** to taste

Makes 9 servings
Calories: 185 per serving

Pour 5 ½ cups of water in a slow cooker over low heat. Add the bouillon cube and stir until dissolved.

Add the rest of the ingredients to the cooker, stir, cover, and continue cooking on low heat for 7 hours. At this point, the peas should be tender.

Enjoy!

Section 5: Desserts

1. Multi-Layered Coconut Brownies

These brownies are delicious and fulfilling and count among my favorite desserts. The coconut ingredients add a distinct flavor and have a lot of health benefits.

¼ cup gluten-free **oats**
16 oz. (450 g) gluten-free **brownie mix**
¼ cup **butter** or **coconut butter**
1 **egg**
1 can sweetened **milk** or **coconut milk**
¼ cup **coconut flakes**
¼ cup **walnuts**

Makes 8 servings
Calories: 95 per serving

Melt the butter of your choice in a slow cooker over medium heat. Add ¼ cup of water, the brownie mix and egg, then stir to mix.

Add the milk of your choice to the cooker, then cover with coconut flakes, walnut, and oats.

Cover and set heat to high and cook for 2 ¼ hours. Insert a knife and see if it comes out clean. If it does, remove the cover and cook for 15 more minutes. If the knife does not come out clean, continue cooking and test periodically. In mini slow cookers, it can take up to 4 hours.

Enjoy!

2. Vanilla Peaches or Apples

This recipe is simple but amazing. One of its finest qualities is the smell of cinnamon and cloves that will spread through your house.

8 **peaches** or 4 **apples** (sliced)
½ tsp **cinnamon** (ground)
½ tsp **cloves** (ground)
1/4 cup **butter** or **coconut butter**
1 cup **sugar**
1 scoop **vanilla ice cream**

Makes 8 servings
Calories: 85 per serving

Place the peaches or apples, cloves, cinnamon, sugar and the butter of your choice in a slow cooker. Stir to mix. Cover, set heat to low and cook for 2 hours.

Top with 1 scoop of vanilla ice cream and serve hot.

Enjoy!

3. Nutty Coconut Rice Pudding

Rice is not only good for meals of many varieties, it also works well in desserts. This one is unforgettable. It combines vanilla, almond and coconut flavor.

½ cup **rice** (white, brown or basmati)
14 oz. (400 ml) **coconut milk**
¼ cup **coconut meat** (shredded)
1 cup **almond milk**
¼ cup **almonds** (chopped, toasted)
¼ tsp **almond extract** (ground)
½ tsp **vanilla extract**
½ tsp **cinnamon** (ground)
½ cup **raisins**
¼ tsp **nutmeg** (ground)
¼ cup **honey** or **agave nectar**
1/3 cup **water**

Makes 5 servings
Calories: 90 per serving

Place the rice of your choice, coconut milk, vanilla extract, almond milk, almond extract, nutmeg, and cinnamon in a slow cooker.

Cover, set heat to low and cook for 4 hours, or 2 ½ hours on high heat.

At the end, stir in the almonds, coconut meat and raisins. Drizzle with honey or agave nectar and serve.

Enjoy!

4. Lemon Blueberry Cake

Baking a cake in a slow cooker instead of the oven is a new concept for many. There are two advantages of using a slow cooker for this: It only takes 1-2 hours to bake the cake and it uses *much* less electricity.

½ cup **arrowroot flour** or **coconut flour**
¼ tsp gluten-free **baking powder**
¼ tsp **stevia**
1 tsp **olive oil** or **coconut oil**
¼ tsp **lemon extract**
½ tsp **lemon zest**
¼ tsp **vanilla extract**
⅓ cup **milk** or **coconut milk**
¼ cup **blueberries**
1 tsp **flaxseeds** (ground)
1 tsp **agave nectar** or **honey** to taste

Makes 4 servings
Calories: 85 per serving

Coat a slow cooker with the oil of your choice. Add the flour of your choice, baking powder, stevia, and either honey or agave nectar.

Add the milk of your choice, blueberries, flaxseeds, lemon zest, lemon extract, and vanilla extract to the cooker. Stir to mix and spread evenly.

Cover and set heat to high, then cook for 1 hour and 10 minutes. At this point, the middle of the cake should be solid.

Serve and enjoy!

5. Berry Cobbler

Cobbler is a great type of dessert, and there are many ways to make it. This one is a family favorite.

1 cup **arrowroot flour** or **coconut flour**
1 tsp gluten-free **baking powder**
¼ tsp **cinnamon**
1 **egg**
¼ cup **milk** or **coconut milk**
2 tbs **olive oil** or **coconut oil**
2 cups **raspberries**
2 cups **blueberries**
½ tbs **lemon juice**
1 cup + 3 tbs **sugar**
1 scoop **ice cream** or **yoghurt** (optional)
1/8 tsp **salt**

Makes 8 servings
Calories: 95 per serving

Place the flour of your choice, cinnamon, 3 tbs sugar, baking powder, egg, and the milk and oil of your choice in a slow cooker. Whisk to blend.

In a bowl, combine ¼ cup of your chosen flour, salt, and 1 cup sugar. Add the blueberries, raspberries, and lemon juice. Stir to coat.

Top the batter in the slow cooker with the berry mix. Make sure it is evenly distributed.

Cover, set heat to low and cook for 2 hours and 15 minutes. At this point, the batter should be cooked through.

Optionally, top with 1 scoop of frozen yogurt or ice cream of any flavor.

Made in the USA
Las Vegas, NV
04 January 2024

83931566R00036